JAMES GEDDY
and SONS
Colonial Craftsmen

Colonial Williamsburg Archaeological Series No. 5

JAMES GEDDY
and SONS
Colonial Craftsmen

by

IVOR NOËL HUME

Published by
THE COLONIAL WILLIAMSBURG FOUNDATION
Williamsburg, Virginia

PREFACE

The details of an archaeological excavation are rarely of interest to anyone other than those directly concerned with the site and with the digging. For the rest of us only the end product matters, specifically the answers to the questions – what was found and what conclusions were drawn from it? Nothing up to that point is any more intriguing than are the rough figures leading to the solution of a mathematical problem. Because this series of publications is intended to be both useful and attractive to a much wider audience than will ever think of the James Geddy House in archaeological terms, the text is devoted mainly to the excavations' principal contribution–the assembling of a unique collection of artifacts associated with the colonial gunsmithing, brass-founding, and silversmithing crafts.

Consequently, the archaeological history of the house has been omitted; so, too, has all information relating to the family's domestic life. However, some of the interesting ceramics from the site are illustrated in Volume 2 of this series, *Pottery and Porcelain in Colonial Williamsburg's Archaeological Collections* (*Figures 9, 14, 25, 33, and 36*).

For the benefit of those who may wish to use the illustrated artifacts for comparative purposes or who need to cite them as parallels in their own publications, the catalog number and principal measurements of each item are listed on pages 43, 44, and 45. In those instances where the presence of a scale is important to an even cursory interpretation of the photographs a one-inch pin has been included in the picture.

I.N.H.

February 1970

JAMES GEDDY
and SONS
Colonial Craftsmen

FIGURE 1
The James Geddy House as it was in 1929, before restoration.

FIGURE 2
The yard and rear of the Geddy House after completion of the 1968 excavations but before reconstruction of the smaller outbuildings and the replacement of the shed addition to the rear of the house.

IN December 1927, acting on behalf of Mr. John D. Rockefeller Jr., Dr. W.A.R. Goodwin purchased the buildings and lot on the northeast corner of Duke of Gloucester Street and Palace Green, a property then known as the Neale House (*Figure 1*). When he did so, it was realized that the house was old and presumably colonial, but exactly how old and colonial no one was prepared to say. No Colonial Williamsburg research department then existed to explore the property's documentary history; indeed, there was no Colonial Williamsburg. Not until February of the following year was the project officially incorporated under that name.

In 1930, the same year that the massive archaeological study of the Governor's Palace site was in progress at the other end of the green, the first digging began around the Neale House. The excavations were limited to locating a kitchen foundation and to the examination of such details as porches, bulkheads, and walkways leading to the house. This done, those parts of the building that were considered to date from the nineteenth century or to be even later additions were removed and the house restored to its colonial appearance. While these archaeological and architectural studies were going on, it was found that the house had been part of a larger complex that included both a shop and a rental property to the east. Twenty-two years later, when these were reconstructed, further archaeological digging took place. On each occasion this work was motivated by the need to obtain information to help the architects re-create the original appearance of the house and its appendages. Although the excavators cut through much accumulated soil rich in colonial artifacts, no attempt was made to extend the digging to explore ground that was not thought to contain evidence pertinent to the architectural story.

This reluctance on the part of the archaeologists to disturb ground that did not seem to contain answers to the questions they were asking proved to be a blessing. It meant that much of the site remained undisturbed until it could be subjected to a more critical examination made possible by modern advances in archaeological techniques. Thus the third excavation of the site was deferred until 1968 when a great deal more was known both about the artifacts of the period and about the history of the James Geddy House itself.

FIGURE 3
Plan of the brass founder's workshop in the yard to the rear of the Geddy House. The cross-hatching denotes foundations of a workroom added after the sale of lot 162 necessitating relinquishing the east room to the new owner.

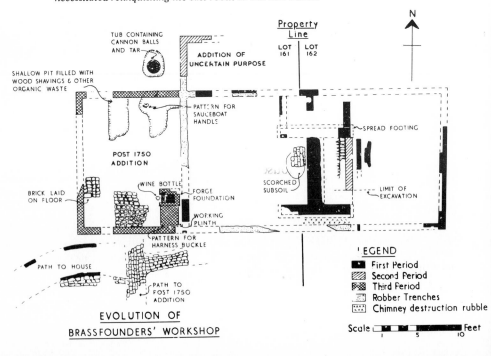

EVOLUTION OF
BRASSFOUNDERS' WORKSHOP

The excavations that yielded the artifacts illustrated here extended all around the restored house and throughout the yard area stretching northward from it to the reconstructed outbuildings. As the Geddy family had also owned lot No. 162 to the east, the digging went far enough in that direction to expose the ground plan of a brass-working shop whose foundations spanned the property line between the two lots (*Figure 3*).

The first James Geddy was a gunsmith and brass founder who was already established on the east lot when he bought its neighbor, lot No. 161, to the west in 1738. In October of that year he advertised that he could provide the *Virginia Gazette's* subscribers with "neat Fowling-Pieces, and large Guns fit for killing Wild-Fowl in Rivers." He added that he also made "several Sorts of wrought Brass-work, and casts small Bells."[1] Further evidence of the extent of his work was provided by another advertisement, of October 1739, wherein James Geddy described a gun that had been brought to his shop "to be new Stock'd and Lock'd,"[2] indicating that he did not confine his work to the metal parts.

Geddy died in 1744 leaving most of his estate to his widow, Anne, along with bequests to four sons and three daughters. The sons were cited in the following order: David, James, William, and John, presumably in order of seniority. Nothing is known about the family's activities on the property in the years immediately thereafter, but thanks to yet another advertisement, of 1751, we learn that David and William went into partnership continuing their father's dual trades of gunsmithing and brass-founding.[3] The notice in the *Virginia Gazette* is long and extremely informative:

> DAVID and WILLIAM GEDDY Smiths in *Williamsburg,*
> near the Church, having all Manner of Utensils requisite,
> carry on the Gunsmith's, Cutler's, and Founder's Trade, at
> whose Shop may be had the following Work, *viz.* Gun

1. *Virginia Gazette,* October 6, 1738.

2. *Ibid.,* October 5, 1739.

3. It should be noted that the title of this publication is not intended to indicate that the first James Geddy and his sons were ever in partnership or that they were in business under the name James Geddy & Sons. However, such a formal partnership did exist in 1791 between James Geddy II, James Geddy III, and William Waddill Geddy.

FIGURE 4a
The furnace in the workshop's west addition in course of excavation. Note the body of a wine bottle of about 1730 lying in the mouth of the ash box.

FIGURE 4b
The bottle reunited with its neck after the latter was found amid ashes beneath the furnace grating.

12

Work, such as Guns and Pistols Stocks, plain or neatly varnished, Locks and Mountings, Barrels, blued, bored, and rifled; Founder's Work, and Harness Buckles, Coach Knobs, Hinges, Squares, Nails and Bullions, curious Brass Fenders and Fire Dogs, House Bells of all Sizes, Dials calculated to any Latitude; Cutler's Work, as Razors, Lancets, Shears, and Surgeon's Instruments ground, cleaned, and glazed, as well as when first made, Sword Blades polished, blued, and gilt in the neatest Manner, Scabbards for Swords, Needles and Sights for Surveyors Compasses, Rupture Bands of different Sorts, particularly a Sort which gives admirable Ease in all Kinds of Ruptures; Likewise at the said Shop may be had a Vermifuge, Price, *3s. 6d. per* Bottle, which safely and effectually destroys all Kinds of Worms in Horses, the most inveterate Pole-evils and Fistulas cured, and all Diseases incident to Horses; at their said Shop.[4]

When one realizes that in eighteenth-century London the trades of gunsmith, brass founder, bucklemaker, cutler, and swordsmith were often pursued by separate individuals, it is evident that the Geddy brothers were young men of varied accomplishments. Nevertheless, this versatility did not result in an expansion of their late father's premises; on the contrary, in 1750 their mother elected to sell the east property (lot 162) and so apparently squeezed both the living and working accommodations onto lot 161. It was a decision that had a drastic effect on the lot-straddling workshop whose east room had to be vacated and its furnace replaced by another in a new workroom added to the west end of the building (*Figure 4a*).

---

4. *Ibid.*, August 8, 1751.

FIGURE 4c
An illustration from Denis Diderot's encyclopedia (Plates, vol. VIII, 1771) showing a goldsmith's small forge with features and proportions comparable to those of the Geddy example.

 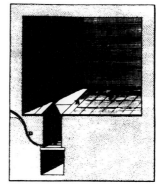

During excavations beneath the extant James Geddy House the remains of another building were found, a building which also possessed a furnace foundation attached to a wing addition (*Figure 5*). The archaeological evidence suggested that when James Geddy I first set up in business in Williamsburg he lived on lot 162 and then established his shop and forge in a building on the site of the present dwelling. Indeed, there was little doubt that Geddy was involved with construction work on that westerly lot, as part of a wine bottle engraved with his initials was found in a trench beside one of the early foundations (*Figure 6*).

It is probable that shortly before Mrs. Geddy sold lot 162, she had the old building and workshop addition on the corner of Duke of Gloucester Street and Palace Green taken down and a new house built on the same site. In August 1760 she conveyed the house and lot to her son James Geddy who was identified in the deed as a "Silver Smith."[5] A month later James leased a tenement attached to the east end of the dwelling to Messrs. Walker and Goode, merchants, for a period of fifteen years and gave them permission to make extensive improvements to it. At some time, probably on more than one occasion between 1760 and 1770, the younger James Geddy made changes of his own to the house. Exactly how extensive those changes were remains in doubt, but they certainly entailed attaching a lean-to addition to the rear of the house and projecting the bulkhead entrance out beyond it. The lean-to roof probably reached right across the back of the building and abutted a shed addition known to have been built by Walker and Goode.

In 1777 James Geddy II offered his property for sale, and at that time he described it as comprising "THE houses and lot whereon I now live in *Williamsburg*, well improved, and the whole built within these few years."[6] The meaning of the last phrase has been a source of much speculation. The archaeological evidence indicates that James Geddy had made several changes in the property about 1770. These included digging a cellar beneath the northwest wing, removing the old brass-founding shop and

---

5. York County Records, Deeds, VI, pp. 276-278.
6. *Virginia Gazette* (Purdie), May 2, 1777.

FIGURE 5
Foundation of the north wall of the first Geddy house across the foreground, and beyond it the east wall of the added wing that was later cut through by the construction of a brick-based forge.

FIGURE 6
Detail of a fragmentary wine bottle of about 1730 engraved with the initials JG and found in the builder's trench beside a footing within the earliest house foundation.

FIGURE 7
The second of three well shafts found on the Geddy property, this example filled with rubbish after the side collapsed about 1765. The brick-edged stone slab beyond the well may have served as a footing for a water barrel.

FIGURE 8
The virtually intact fire box and the outline of the robbed foundation for a smokehouse believed to have been built by James Geddy about 1770. The building was approached by a brick path from the south, the bricks, of the tapered "compass" type, apparently left over from lining the adjacent well shaft. Note the collection of broken wine bottles in the left foreground corner of the smokehouse.

constructing a dairy in its place, dismantling an old kitchen and building a new one, digging a new well, and building a smokehouse (*Figures 7 and 8*). Whether he also rebuilt the dwelling house was beyond the capacity of archaeology to determine.

There is no knowing what became of David Geddy, his name being absent from the surviving records after the advertisement of 1751, but his brother William remained in Williamsburg into the 1760s, though apparently owning no property. He made purchases of scrap brass in 1763 and so it is reasonable to conclude that he was still casting brassware, if only for making guns. There is both archaeological and documentary evidence to suggest that gun-smithing was William's primary occupation. On the other hand, two small brass furniture hooks one or both stamped with the initials "D G" were found in the excavations suggesting, perhaps, that David Geddy was the family's principal worker in brass (*Figure 9*).

In January 1776 William reappeared in the records as being paid by the Committee of Safety for "Casting ball, repairing Arms &c.," and during the spring of that year he was paid for guns both sold and repaired.[7] The records do not reveal where he did this, but the archaeological discoveries strongly point to his having been working behind his brother James's house. Along with a broad spread of iron-working refuse, a shallow pit was found there containing a large quantity of slag and iron scraps, as well as discarded and unfinished gun parts. The date of this deposit was revealed by the discovery of fragments of Governor Dunmore's Chinese porcelain armorial dinner service which may well have been removed from the Palace by souvenir collectors on one of the three occasions that the building was broken into between June 24 and July 12, 1775, the last of which caused His Lordship to complain that "my house has been a third time rifled, and is now entirely in the possession of these lawless Ruffians."[8] Further dating evidence was provided by the inclusion in the pit of French

---

7. Account for General Expenses of the Army. Committee of Safety Ledger 1775-1776, p. 38.

8. Dunmore to Dartmouth, July 12, 1775, C. O. 5/1353, Public Records Office, illustrated as *Figure 41* in Ivor Noël Hume, *Pottery and Porcelain in Colonial Williamsburg's Archaeological Collections.*

FIGURE 9
Brass furniture hooks with maker's stamps, the lower example clearly marked DG and the upper with the letter D barely identifiable. It is possible, even likely, that both were made in the shop of David Geddy.

FIGURE 10
Examples of gunlock plates (exterior faces) discarded in the course of the Geddy family's gunsmithing work. Although associated with artifacts of the period 1740-50, the early doglock (1) was found in a layer sealed by gunsmithing waste of the Revolutionary period. Doglocks of this type are attributable to a date as early as the 1640s, but it is likely that this specimen, and the example below it (2), were removed from guns being refurbished in 1775 or 1776 for use by the Patriot forces. The regular flintlock plates (3 and 4) were both recovered from the Revolutionary period gunsmithing debris.

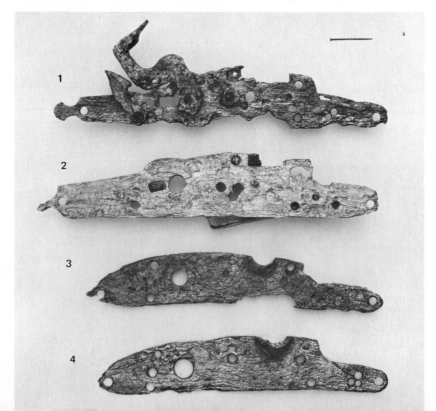

faience that was not legally imported in trade into Virginia before the beginning of the Revolutionary War.

The documentary records leave no doubt that many of the weapons available to the Patriot forces were old, but there had been few opportunities to discover just how old they could be until the abandoned parts were found behind the Geddy House. Two of the firing mechanisms were of doglock type and dated back to the 1640s, while an intact matchlock represented the earliest and most primitive mechanism of all *(Figures 10 and 11)*. Presumably all three had been removed from otherwise usable guns that were then modernized with flintlocks.

Evidence that William Geddy (if, indeed, it was he) was also casting in brass while working on the Patriot guns was provided

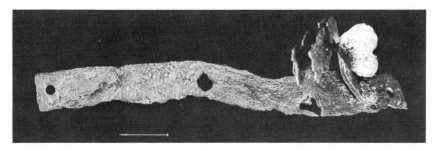

FIGURE 11
Matchlock with serpentine cock and heart-shaped head to its screw. The type dates back to the sixteenth century, but it is known that forty-six guns described as "Match locks new" were listed as being in the magazine at Middle Plantation (later Williamsburg) in 1682/3. The illustrated example was found amid the Revolutionary period gunsmithing waste behind the James Geddy House.

FIGURE 12
Examples of eighteenth-century gunlocks (interior faces). Nos. 1 and 2 are from a rubbish pit sealed in about 1760, and No. 3 from the ca. 1775-1776 Revolutionary gunsmithing debris. No. 1 probably comes from a sporting gun, and Nos. 2 and 3 are types used on military muskets of the first half of the eighteenth century.

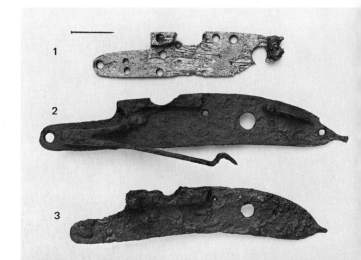

by the presence amid the musket parts of the rough casting for a brass baldric buckle (*Figure 14*).[9] Gunsmithing also entailed brass casting and the relics of this work found on the site included lead patterns used for casting side plates and trigger guards (*Figure 15*). Those were pressed into the sand molds and then removed to leave the impressions into which the molten brass would run. Sometimes the metal declined to flow properly or the impressions were damaged before it was poured, and as a result the rough castings emerged either incomplete or in the wrong shape. As a rule these spoiled products were remelted and used again; but over the years numerous pieces were lost, and from among those that turned up in the excavations it has been possible to determine the shapes of

---

9. A baldric was a broad strap slung over a soldier's shoulder and across his chest to support a sword, bugle, or bayonet frog.

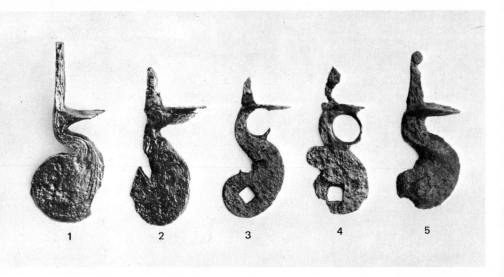

FIGURE 13
Cocks from gunlocks, all save one from the Revolutionary period gunsmith's waste. The example on the extreme left is unfinished; No. 2 is a dog cock of a type dating no later than about 1720; No. 3 is of the throat-hole type (as in No. 4) and has been braised below the neck; and No. 4 has a curious and seemingly unparalleled hump behind its neck. No. 5 has no unusual features and comes from an archaeological context of about 1760.

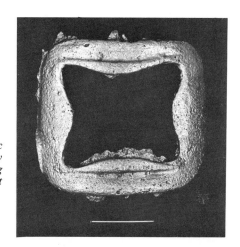

FIGURE 14
Rough casting in brass for a baldric buckle found amid the Revolutionary period gunsmith's waste and suggesting that he manufactured other equipment needed by the Patriot forces.

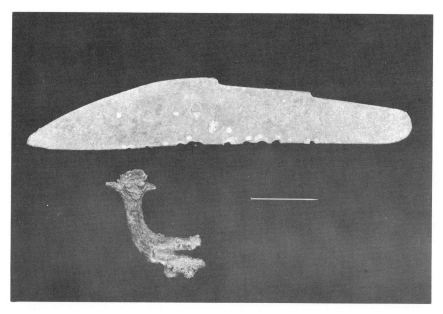

FIGURE 15
Lead pattern to be pressed into a sand mold for casting the side plate for a musket; below, part of the lead pattern for casting a trigger guard, the latter found buried in the workshop floor along with the handle pattern illustrated in Figure 19. *Both gun patterns were discarded around 1750.*

some of the trigger plates, side plates, and gun escutcheons made in the Geddy workshop (*Figures 16 and 17*).

Evidence of the Geddy family's brass working was by no means confined to gun parts; the lead patterns included those for shaping coach studs, harness rings, and buckles both small and large (*Figure 18*). The largest buckle pattern was found jammed between the workshop wall and the brick plinth at the side of the furnace where it had slipped at some date between 1750 and

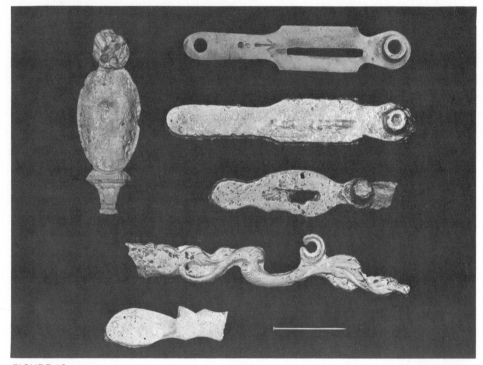

FIGURE 16

Spoiled castings for brass gun furniture. At left an escutcheon for a sporting gun, the central shield having sunk in the middle over the undrilled mounting sleeve. To the right are two trigger plates, that at the top a typical Brown Bess specimen (not from the site) and under it a rough casting of comparable type found in the excavations. Below the latter is another unfinished casting for a trigger plate, this one for use on a pistol. Part of the sprue to which the plate was anchored can be seen to the right of the mounting screw sleeve. Also shown is a spoiled casting for an ornamental side plate, the decoration and left screw hole blocked in, and sprue extending beyond it. Below and to the left is a partially trimmed casting that may also have been intended for a side plate. With the exception of the escutcheon plate which was found in the topsoil, all the excavated items come from contexts dating around 1750-1760.

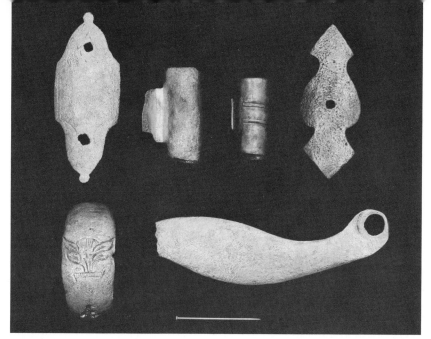

FIGURE 17

Gun furniture: At top left and right, crudely made escutcheons; between them thimbles to hold ramrods; at bottom left an engraved trigger guard for a pistol; and at right part of a plain side plate, probably removed from a French infantry musket. All are brass with the exception of the left thimble that was cut from thin sheet copper. Both thimbles come from archaeological contexts of the mid-eighteenth century. The trigger guard was found in another of about 1770, and the remaining items were found in the topsoil. However, the left escutcheon is closely paralleled by one on an American-made fowler dating from the 1750s.

FIGURE 18

Patterns for buckles and harness rings: At top left, a lead pattern for a harness buckle, found in the space between wall and forge in the brass founders' workshop. To the right is a smaller buckle pattern of lead, and beside it an uncleaned brass buckle derived from it and spoiled in the casting. Below is the lead pattern for a harness ring, and alongside it a brass ring with shape idiosyncrasies similar to those of the pattern. Although the pattern was found near the Geddy workshop, the ring was found on property owned by glazier James Wray near the College of William and Mary. All are from archaeological contexts dating no earlier than the 1750s.

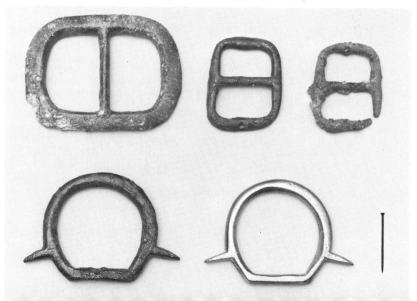

about 1770 when the shop is believed to have been pulled down. Found in a shallow trough in the floor of the same workshop room was a pattern for a handle that may have been used in shaping castings for silver sauceboats (*Figure 19*). That, plus a small strip of silver found under the lean-to room on the back of James Geddy's house, was the only identifiable relic of silver-smithing from the site. This negative evidence, coupled with the wording of his many newspaper advertisements, may suggest that James Geddy did less manufacturing than selling of imported or other American craftsmen's silver, and that much of his business was devoted to the sale of jewelry, shoe buckles, spurs, seals, buttons, and so forth, and to the repairing of watches.[10] A typical advertisement reads:

> JAMES GEDDY, GOLDSMITH, *Near the Church in* Williamsburg, *has now on hand for* SALE, *very cheap, for ready money, the following articles,* VIZ. SILVER Tea Spoons and Tongs, Mens, Womens, and Childrens Shoe Buckles, Stock and Knee do. Spurs, Plain and Stone Rings, Stone Seals, Plain and Stone Brooches, Plain and Stone Gold Buttons, Plain and Stone Silver Buttons and Studs, Plain and Stone Earrings in Gold, and many other articles. N.B. He still continues to clean and repair WATCHES, and repairs his own work that fails in a reasonable time, without any expense to the purchaser.[11]

Very often Geddy would say that his wares were "Just imported" on this, that, or the other ship, but it is clear that some items of the kinds listed in the advertisements were made at the shop. Among them were delicately cast watch keys, and shoe buckles of elegant forms hitherto thought to have been British, but all of which were recovered in their unfinished or spoiled states (*Figures 21 and 23*).

Because it quickly became apparent that the Geddy brass founders were capable of making anything from the heaviest brass trunk handles to the most delicate of watch keys, it was tempting to conjecture that any brass object found on the site was made

---

10. When James Geddy II sold his Williamsburg property in 1778, the deed referred to him as "James Geddy—Jeweller of Dinwiddie." York County Records, Deeds, VI, p. 48.
11. *Virginia Gazette* (Purdie and Dixon), March 5, 1767.

FIGURE 19

At the left is a lead pattern, possibly for the handle of a silver sauceboat, found in a hole in the floor of the brass founders' workshop. At the right, an anchor of lead, possibly a pattern; found on the adjacent colonial lot, No. 162, which was sold by Mrs. Geddy in 1750.

FIGURE 20

Spoiled and finished castings for brass harness ornaments; that above was found along with the trigger guard and handle patterns (Figures 15 and 19) in the floor of the Geddy workshop, while the matching completed example was found at the Archibald Blair stables.

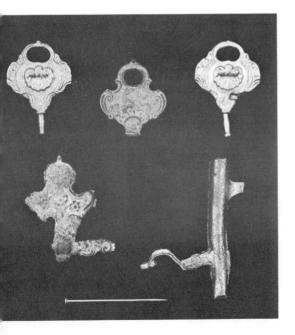

FIGURE 21

Watch keys: At top left and right are terminals with pintels from the same mold; they were found in archaeological contexts associating them with the copper sprue at bottom right. The latter has part of what may be a watch key still attached to it. All were thrown away around 1770. At the top center is an elaborately decorated terminal for either a seal or a pivoting key but which has not been cast or drilled to take a post, while at lower left is part of a finished pivoting key, gilded and with floral decoration. Both examples are believed to date from the third quarter of the eighteenth century, and all the keys are of brass.

25

FIGURE 22
Blue glass intaglio from a seal of a kind that James Geddy II may have included in his jewelry stock. The portrait has not been identified but the dress appears to be of the late sixteenth century, and it is possible that the bust is that of an Elizabethan literary figure. Unfortunately, the seal comes from a disturbed archaeological context and cannot be accurately dated.

FIGURE 23
Unfinished copper-alloy frames for Geddy-made shoe buckles. Neither example has been drilled to receive its central pivot, while that on the left was in the process of receiving additional hand tooling to provide four rosettes or stars. The rosette at right has been completed, that at the left was started, but the blanks at top and bottom had not been touched. Both buckles are of types popular in the third quarter of the eighteenth century.

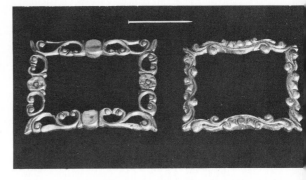

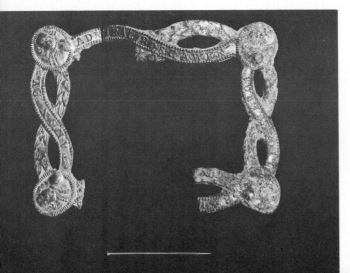

FIGURE 24
Part of a silver-plated copper shoe buckle frame made to commemorate the capture of Louisbourg in Nova Scotia in 1758, and decorated with portraits of Admiral Boscawen (see p. 27).

there. This was particularly so of one of the shoe buckles which has strong American historical associations, a plated copper buckle decorated in its corners with four portraits of the British admiral who captured the fortress of Louisbourg in Nova Scotia from the French during the Seven Years' War (*Figure 24*). It is inscribed in relief around the edge with the words L[OUISBOURG] TAKEN BY ADMIRAL BOSCAWEN JULY THE 26 1758. Because American colonial forces were largely responsible for the victory, it might be argued that this buckle was made at the Geddy shop to capitalize on the admiral's popularity. Unfortunately the buckle was completed and was in no way defective, and therefore such a conclusion would be highly irresponsible. In spite of the irrefutable evidence of the Geddy family's brass-working accomplishments and capabilities, it is safer to assume that all the metal objects were imported unless one can provide proof to the contrary.

Literally hundreds of copper, brass, and tin-plated brass objects were found, including spoons, spurs, thimbles, buttons, buckles, book fittings, harness ornaments, curtain rings, bells, and furniture

FIGURE 25
Latten spoons: Above, fragments of finished spoons not necessarily made on the site; below, part of a bowl that went wrong in the casting and was almost certainly a Geddy product. The finished, tin-plated bowl was discarded in the second quarter of the eighteenth century and the spoiled casting at a date after 1740.

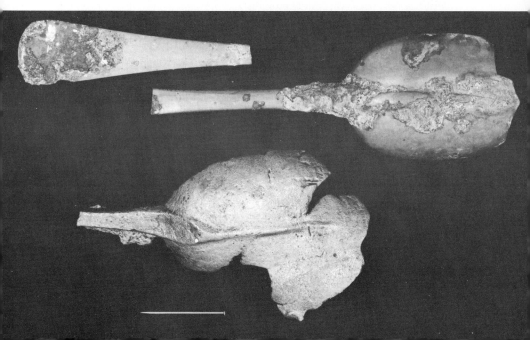

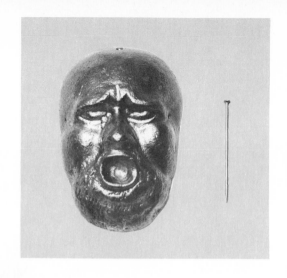

FIGURE 26
Brass mask of uncertain purpose and date. The casting is heavy and there is no visible means of anchoring it, save for a small hole at the top of the head.

FIGURE 27
Part of a brass band originally sewn to a leather dog collar and engraved "JASPer." The first four letters are fairly well executed but the last two seem to have been added in lower case by another hand. The name could be that of the dog, but was more probably that of the owner. A city ordinance of 1772 required that no dog should be kept in Williamsburg "without a Collar worn about his Neck, whereon the initial Letters of the Owner's Christian and Surname shall be marked." This rule superseded an act of Common Council passed in March 1739, the text of which unfortunately does not survive. The collar fragment was discarded no earlier than 1745.

FIGURE 28
Bronze weights of one ounce and half an ounce avoirdupois, perhaps used in weighing components for mixing copper alloys. It is unlikely that they would have been used by the silversmith, as precious metals were weighed in troy ounces. The one-ounce specimen is marked with a crowned G indicating that it dates from the reign of George I, II, or III. The large A probably denotes avoirdupois; the dagger of St. Paul shows that it was made in London; while the ewer is the mark of the Founders' Company that had the right to inspect brass weights used in London and its immediate environs. The half-ounce weight was found on lot 162 which Mrs. Geddy sold in 1750, and perhaps significantly, this example is the earlier of the two, being stamped with the crowned A initial of Queen Anne.

FIGURE 29
*A sword blade with its tang rolled over, presumably to be used as scrap metal. The blade comes from a context dating after 1760, a deposit that also contained part of a brass knuckle bow for a sword hilt (*see Figure 30*).*

FIGURE 30
A sword assembled from components found on the Geddy site, all save the pommel having archaeological associations dating their abandonment to the third quarter of the eighteenth century.

ornaments. Although some of them parallel items listed in David
and William Geddy's 1751 advertisement, there is no proof that
most of these excavated examples were their products. Nevertheless, there is a sufficient number of undeniably Geddy-made items
from the site to illustrate most of the categories described in the
1751 notice.

The evidence of gunsmithing has already been discussed as has
that for the casting of harness buckles. In some instances the
archaeological evidence went further than the documentary. Thus,
for example, David and William advertised only that they could
offer "Sword Blades polished, blued, and gilt in the neatest
Manner"; they said nothing about making swords. However,
unfinished or reworked blade fragments were unearthed (*Figures
29 and 30*) as were unfinished brass hilt parts, indicating that
swords were either made or put together at the shop. *Figure 31*

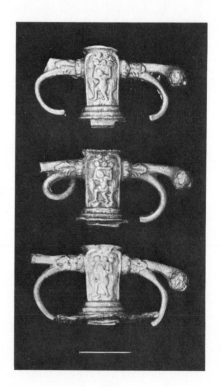

FIGURE 31
*Three brass quillon blocks cast from the
same pattern, and found at the Geddy
site, Governor's Palace, and Wray site
respectively. Both the Geddy and Palace
examples are untrimmed and apparently
unfinished, but the Wray site block has a
cut-down shell guard attached to it, indicating that the block was made up into a
hilt and later dismantled as scrap brass.
Both the Geddy and Wray specimens
come from archaeological contexts dating after 1750.*

shows three quillon blocks from the same mold, one found on the Geddy site, another recovered from excavations at the Governor's Palace in 1930, and the third found on property at the other end of town owned by James Wray, a carpenter and glazier. The block from the Wray site had been assembled into a sword hilt and then chopped apart, suggesting that it reached Mr. Wray in the form of scrap brass. The same may be true of a brass harness fitting from the same site and exactly paralleled by a lead pattern from the Geddy House excavations (*Figure 18*). Although it is possible that the Geddys purchased sword parts in the rough state and finished them at the shop, there is no doubt that the craftsmen were quite capable of manufacturing any or all of these items.

The documentary evidence fails to show whether any member of the Geddy family made clocks or watches, although there are numerous advertisements, such as the one quoted on page 24,

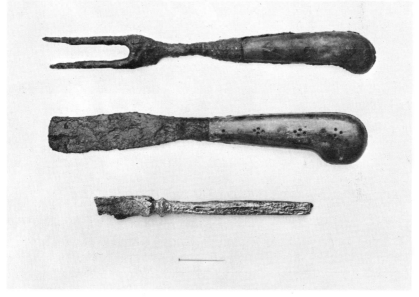

FIGURE 32
*Knife and fork with plated bone handles, both from contexts of the 1760s, and below, the tang and shoulders from an unfinished table knife that had been thrown into a well abandoned in the same period (*see Figure 7*).*

wherein James Geddy offered to clean and repair watches. However, in addition to the watch keys previously mentioned, many fragments of broken watch glasses were found in the yard behind the house.

As a rule, watchmakers also made clocks, and although James Geddy never mentioned clocks in his advertisements, two incomplete spandrel castings (the ornamental corners attached to clock dials) were found (*Figure 34*). One of them is represented only by the head of a cherub, but the other is virtually complete and is of a type that occurs on clocks made in and around Philadelphia in the second and third quarters of the eighteenth century. Indeed, the unfinished Geddy example exhibits the same pattern flaws as an example on a clock made by the famous Philadelphia maker, Peter Stretch, who died in 1746. Spandrels of the same type also occur on a clock by another Philadelphia maker, John Wood (d.1761), who purchased Peter Stretch's shop. Another surviving clock with similar spandrels was made by Isaac Pearson who

FIGURE 33
Whetstones: Those at left and right are of granite, the center example of sandstone. These may have been used in the Geddy family's swordsmithing and cutlery work.

FIGURE 34

Rough castings for spandrels used to decorate the faces of clocks. The cherub's face has been cut from the center of a spandrel of comparable size to the intact specimen. That it was never finished is proved by the fact that the rivet hole above the head has not been drilled out. The almost complete specimen with its cherubs supporting a crown is just as it came from the mold, none of the excess brass having been trimmed and none of the holes drilled (see p. 32). The latter spandrel was found in a context of about 1775, while the trimmed cherub is from another of about 1760.

FIGURE 35

Crucibles: The largest example is marked 5 TM in lettering comparable to that on another, slightly larger, specimen (not shown) stamped 6 TM. The smallest of these illustrated crucibles, though unused, is paralleled by fragments of two others having drops of gold adhering to them. The much-used base at right is coated with dross and contains traces of copper. The specimen at the left rear is of a type known in the eighteenth century as a "black lead crucible" (black lead meaning graphite). Crucibles of this material were being made in Philadelphia in 1774 and were said to have been "found to be much better than any imported." The other illustrated specimens are of hard-fired earthenware made from potters' clay, fine sand, and ground up old crucibles or stoneware sherds.

FIGURE 36

Examples of brass sprue from the pouring channels of sand molds, the arms originally attached to the molded castings. Mid-eighteenth century.

worked at Burlington, New Jersey, until his death in 1749. The village of Burlington was only a few miles northeast of Philadelphia on the Delaware river. A fourth clock with comparable ornaments was made by Benjamin Chandlee, Jr., of Nottingham, Pennsylvania, and is dated 1774. However, it is believed that the clock was put together using pieces from the workshop of Benjamin Chandlee, Sr., who died in 1745.

The crowned spandrel is considered rare on American clocks, and it is curious therefore that so many virtually identical ornaments should occur in the Philadelphia area with histories connecting them one way or another with the 1740s, and that a comparable unfinished casting should turn up at the Geddy shop

FIGURE 37
Silver teaspoons found in a sand-filled hollow between the well and kitchen and lost in the 1770s. The two specimens on the left are stamped I·G and can reasonably be claimed to be the work of James Geddy II. The third spoon is unmarked, and the fourth is stamped B·H and bears the owner's engraved initials RS, but neither maker nor owner has been identified.

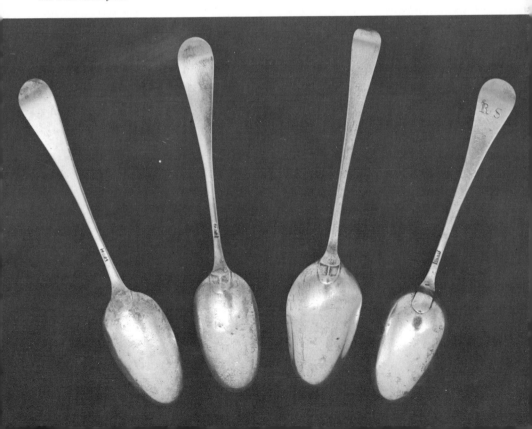

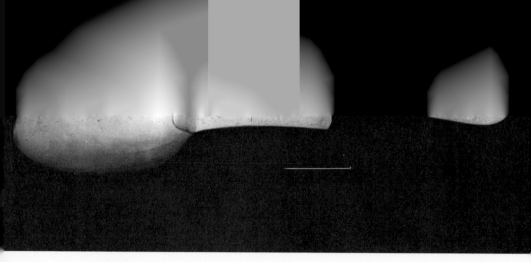

FIGURE 38

Tablespoon engraved with the initials I ^{G} E and the number 12. The initials are almost certainly those of James and Elizabeth Geddy, and the 12 may indicate the place of this spoon in James Geddy's household inventory. The spoon had been broken and repaired with a solder having a high brass content from which copper salts leached in the ground, causing the repair to come apart. The spoon has no maker's mark, but was in use within the period 1760-1777.

site in a context dating around 1775. There are various possible explanations, the least convincing of them being that the Philadelphia spandrels were cast in the Geddy shop. More plausible is the possibility that the Geddys obtained their pattern from the same manufacturer as did Benjamin Chandlee, Jr., though that would not account for the casting idiosyncrasies that are common only to the Williamsburg and Peter Stretch examples. More believable still is the possibility that someone in Williamsburg owned a clock by Stretch, that one of the spandrels was broken or lost, and that it was brought to the Geddy shop for repair. The craftsman then removed one of the remaining spandrels and used it as a pattern to cast the replacement.

Although the excavation had been launched in the hope that it would reveal new information about James Geddy II's silver-smithing, relatively little was forthcoming. Naturally enough, silversmiths were not as careless with their waste products as were brass founders with theirs. Nevertheless, no fewer than five silver spoons were recovered, all of them from a sandfilled depression between the well and the kitchen. Four are teaspoons, two stamped with James Geddy II's "I·G" mark, one marked "B·H" and engraved "RS," and the fourth with no mark at all (*Figure*

37). The two "I•G" marks proved to be identical to that on a teaspoon found on the site of the Governor's Palace in 1930 and engraved with the initials of Christopher and Anne Ayscough, who were Governor Fauquier's gardener and housekeeper until his death in 1768.[12] It had long been assumed that the spoon was a Geddy product, but as there were other American silversmiths with the same initials, the point was not proved until the matching examples were found on the Geddy site.

James Geddy II's advertisement shows that he sold "country made" gold and silver work, meaning that the pieces were made in America but not necessarily by him. He also advertised that he would take old silver "in Exchange for new Work at 7s. per

12. Ivor Noël Hume, *Here Lies Virginia*. New York, 1963, pp. 112-13.

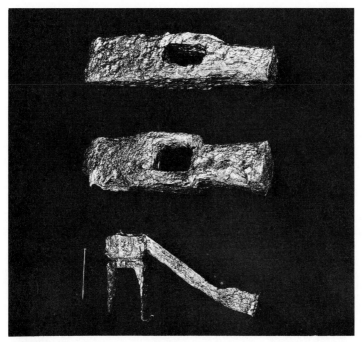

FIGURE 39
Examples of metalsmith's or carpenter's riveting hammer heads and a race knife, all discarded in the mid-eighteenth century. Both hammers have tempered reinforcements to their faces and peens.

FIGURE 40

Files were made from high quality steel, and metal from those that wore out was frequently reused. The example at the top is seen in the process of being beaten into a new shape; that at the left has been cut with a chisel and looped over at one end; while the specimens at right and center have been fashioned into cold chisels. All are from archaeological contexts of the mid-eighteenth century.

FIGURE 41

It is not known whether the Geddy family made locks, though many lock parts were found. But there can be little doubt that iron keys were made on the site as is evidenced by the two unfinished blanks recovered from contexts dating from the third quarter of the eighteenth century.

FIGURE 42
*The archaeological evidence would sug-
gest that the Geddy family was capable
of making a wide variety of useful and
decorative objects from iron or brass.
This now-footless iron candlestick with
its brass reinforcing band was found in
the east room of the brass founders'
workshop in debris deposited in or
shortly after 1750, when the room
ceased to serve that purpose.*

FIGURE 43
*Part of an iron sow bearing the molded inscription BATSTo. This was undoubtedly a
product of the Batsto iron works in New Jersey which was established in 1766. The
fragment, which weighs 34 pounds, was probably left behind when James or William
Geddy moved away from the property, for it was found in the filling over cellar steps
abandoned about 1820.*

Ounce."[13] It is quite possible, therefore, that the unmarked and "B·H" (an unidentified maker) spoons represented old silver brought to the shop for reworking. It is interesting to note that in 1775 James Geddy charged Williamsburg merchant Robert Prentis ten shillings for "6 Spoons to be made up [into] a pr buckles,"[14] and that Colonial Williamsburg's silversmith estimates that six teaspoons like those found at the Geddy site could be reworked to make frames for one pair of shoe buckles.

The fifth of the excavated spoons, a tablespoon, bears no maker's mark but is engraved ✝$\frac{G}{12}$E, the same initials as those of James Geddy II and his wife Elizabeth (*Figure 38*). However, the "12" is less easily explained, though it may indicate that this spoon was No. 12 in a numbered set. It certainly seems likely that

---

13. *Virginia Gazette* (Purdie and Dixon), October 13, 1774.
14. Robert Prentis memorandum book, 1770-1780, fol. 47, Webb-Prentis Papers, Alderman Library, University of Virginia, Charlottesville.

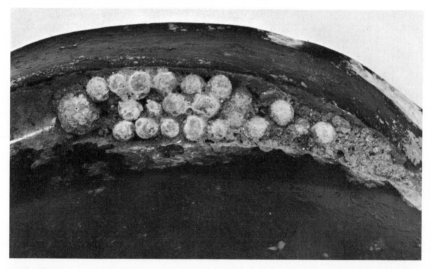

FIGURE 44
The records show that William Geddy cast ammunition for the Patriot troops. These lead pellets, found corroded onto the base of the glass bottle in which they had been stored, were recovered from a context of about 1775. The pellets, however, are bird shot, paralleling the modern No. 5 and BB sizes, and are unlikely to have served any military purpose.

James Geddy would have made his own spoons, but it is equally reasonable to expect that he would have marked them, particularly if he took the trouble to engrave initials and numbers. It is always possible, of course, that the excavated example was made by an apprentice, or perhaps by Geddy before he became a master with the right to his own mark. The spoon is clearly old and very worn; indeed, the handle had broken and had been inexpertly soldered in a repair that came apart in the ground. As this would appear to be the only surviving example of James Geddy's own household silver, one might conclude that he resisted the craftsman's natural desire to keep the best for himself.

No matter how uninspiring a piece of silver may have been, no one would have intentionally thrown it away. Thus the finding of not one but five spoons created a considerable mystery that cannot now be solved. Two possible explanations have been put forward. The first, and perhaps the less likely, is that a servant or apprentice was carrying a box of spoons between kitchen and shop on a wet day, and that he dropped them causing some of the spoons to be lost into a sandy-bottomed puddle beside the well. Not knowing how many spoons were supposed to be in the box, he picked up those that he could see and missed the ones that disappeared into the water. The alternative explanation is that Geddy children amused themselves digging in the sand behind the well and borrowed spoons from the shop with which to do it. Then, as so often happens, the tools got buried and were forgotten when the game was over.

James Geddy II's last surviving advertisement offering the less useful things of colonial life appeared in the *Virginia Gazette* for June 3, 1775. A few days later Governor Dunmore was to flee from Williamsburg leaving the citizens outside the British pale and probably in no mood to invest in Geddy's "genteel assortment of *PLATE* and *JEWELLERY*."[15] Although he advertised in 1776 for old silver, and was acting as a public assayer in October of the next year, it is unlikely that his goldsmithing, silversmithing, and jeweller's business was very profitable once Williamsburg became preoccupied with its preparations for war. By November of 1777

---

15. *Virginia Gazette* (Pinkney), October 13, 1774.

Geddy had moved away from Williamsburg despite the fact that he had been unable to find a purchaser for his property.[16]

The debris of gunsmithing found behind the house provided dramatic evidence of the change that so suddenly came over the city and that marked the beginning of a decline from which Williamsburg never recovered. There is no knowing whether or how much James Geddy involved himself in the gunsmithing operation going on in his backyard, but the scattered slag and iron rubbish leave little doubt that it graphically lowered the tone of his establishment. Perhaps most intriguing of all that martial refuse was a tub buried in the yard north of the old workshop, containing three cannon balls, a quantity of tar, and a feather.

----

16. The house and lot were finally sold on December 11, 1778.

FIGURE 45

A small tub was found buried immediately north of the brass founder's workshop (see Figure 3). It contained three cannon balls, a large quantity of tar, and a feather. The tar remained in its plastic condition as can be seen by the illustrated example. Archaeological data reveal only that the tub was buried after about 1755, but the presence of the cannon balls suggests a Revolutionary date and encourages an obvious, though probably unwise, interpretation for this evocative discovery.

Figure*	*Colonial Williamsburg catalog number*	*Measurements*
4b.	5506. E.R.1337Y–19.B.	Ht. 7 3/4"
6.	5434. E.R.1345J–19.B.	Ht. 4"
9, No. 1.	5509. E.R.1327M–19.B.	Length 1 3/8"
2.	5508. E.R.1327L–19.B.	Length 1 3/4"
10, No. 1.	5398. E.R.1368P–19.B.	Length 8 1/8"
2.	5399. E.R.1329–19.B.	Length 8 1/4"
3.	5400. E.R.1374K–19.B.	Length 7 1/4"
4.	5401. E.R.1346J–19.B.	Length 7"
11.	5573. E.R.1368N–19.B.	Length 7 7/8"
12, No. 1.	5402. E.R.987M–19.B.	Length 4 1/2"
2.	5401. E.R.987M–19.B.	Length 7 1/4"
3.	5403. E.R.1374K–19.B.	Length 6 1/8"
13, No. 1.	5393. E.R.1355V–19.B.	Length 3 1/4"
2.	5396. E.R.1374K–19.B.	Length 3"
3.	5394. E.R.1374K–19.B.	Length 2 7/8"
4.	5397. E.R.1330Y–19.B.	Length 3 1/8"
5.	5395. E.R.1346J–19.B.	Length 3 1/2"
14.	5369. E.R.1374K–19.B.	Width 2 7/8"
15, No. 1.	5493. E.R.1347P–19.B.	Length 6 1/8"
2.	5494. E.R.1350F–19.B.	Ht. 1 3/4"
16, No. 1	5379. E.R.1324A–19.B.	Ht. 3 1/2"
2.	5571–O.C.	Length 3 1/4"
3.	5377. E.R.987N–19.B.	Length 3 3/8"
4.	5378. E.R.1359M–19.B.	Length 2 3/4"
5.	5375. E.R.1359M–19.B.	Length 4 1/4"
6.	5376. E.R.1368N–19.B.	Length 1 3/4"
17, No. 1.	5366. E.R.1344A–19.B.	Length 2 1/8"
2.	5363. E.R.1330Y–19.B.	Ht. 1 1/8"
3.	5364. E.R.1335X–19.B.	Ht. 1"
4.	5365. E.R.1359–19.B.	Length 1 7/8"
5.	5367. E.R.1329F–19.B.	Ht. 1 1/2"
6.	5368. E.R.1323–19.B.	Length 3"
18, No. 1.	5450. E.R.1397L–19.B.	Width 1 7/8"
2.	5451. E.R.1337T–19.B.	Width 1 3/4"
3.	5452. E.R.1379–19.B.	Width 1 3/4"
4.	5453. E.R.1366W–19.B.	Width 2 3/8"
5.	5454. E.R.1216–31.A.	Width 1 3/4"

*All numbering of multiple item illustrations is from left to right and from top to bottom row.

Figure	*Colonial Williamsburg catalog number*	*Measurements*
19, No. 1.	5496. E.R.1350F–19.B.	Width 2 1/4"
2.	5495–19.A.	Ht. 4"
20.	1309–29.H.6.	Width 2"
21, No. 1.	5381. E.R.1324T–19.B.	Length 1"
2.	5384. E.R.1380J–19.B.	Length 3/4"
3.	5382. E.R.1337K–19.B.	Length 1"
4.	5385. E.R.1359H–19.B.	Length 1"
5.	5383. E.R.1337K–19.B.	Length 1 1/2"
22.	5515. E.R.1337A–19.B.	Ht. 3/4"
23, No. 1.	5372. E.R.1353F–19.B.	Width 2"
2.	5373. E.R.1351G–19.B.	Width 1 7/8"
24.	5500. E.R.992D,1380L–19.B.	Width 2 1/2"
25, No. 1.	5510. E.R.1355V–19.B.	Length 3 1/2"
2.	5511. E.R.1377J–19.B.	Length 4 3/4"
3.	5512. E.R.1350H–19.B.	Length 3"
26.	5488. E.R.1359–19.B.	Ht. 1 7/8"
27.	5362. E.R.1321M–19.B.	Length 2 1/4"
28, No. 1.	5634–19.A.	Diam. 1 1/4"
2.	5444. E.R.1362F–19.B.	Diam. 1"
29.	5391. E.R.1380J–19.B.	Blade length 15 1/4" Tang length 5 1/4"
30, No. 1.	Pommel 5389. E.R.1334H–19.B.	Ht. 1 7/8"
2.	Knuckle bow 5390. E.R.1380K–19.B.	Ht. 4 1/4"
3.	Quillon block 5386. E.R.1331F–19.B.	Ht. 1 5/8"
31, No. 1.	5386. E.R.1331F–19.B.	Ht. 1 5/8"
2.	5387–20.A.	Ht. 1 3/8"
3.	5388. E.R.1215–31.A.	Ht. 1 3/8"
32, No. 1.	5436. E.R.1340S–19.B.	Length 7 1/2"
2.	5435. E.R.987M–19.B.	Length 7 1/4"
3.	5437. E.R.1355V–19.B.	Length 4 3/4"
33, No. 1.	5430. E.R.1346B–19.B.	Length 4 5/8"
2.	5432. E.R.1345C–19.B.	Length 3 1/2"
3.	5431. E.R.1366X–19.B.	Length 4 7/16"

Figure	*Colonial Williamsburg catalog number*	*Measurements*
34, No. 1	5370. E.R.1380J – 19.B.	Width 1/2"
2.	5371. E.R.1326F – 19.B.	Ht. 1 1/4"
35, No. 1.	5518. E.R.1340G – 19.B.	Ht. 3 3/4"
2.	5516. E.R.1340V – 19.B.	Ht. 5 1/4"
3.	5519. E.R.1331 – 19.B.	Ht. 1 1/2"
4.	5520. E.R.1340Q – 19.B.	Ht. 2 3/4"
5.	5517. E.R.1362A – 19.B.	Ht. 3 1/4"
36, No. 1.	5491. E.R.1333 – 19.B.	Ht. 3 5/8"
2.	5492. E.R.1359R – 19.B.	Ht. 3 7/8"
37, No. 1.	3811. E.R.1348Q – 19.B.	Length 4 1/4"
2.	3812. E.R.1348Q – 19.B.	Length 4 3/4"
3.	3809. E.R.1352K – 19.B.	Length 4 5/16"
4.	3810. E.R.1352K – 19.B.	Length 4 1/16"
38.	5573. E.R.1352R – 19.B.	Length 8"
39, No. 1.	5433. E.R.1337T – 19.B.	Length 2 1/4"
2.	5637. E.R.1328R – 19.B.	Length 4"
3.	5507. E.R.1359M – 19.B.	Width 3 1/4"
40, No. 1.	5448. E.R.1337T – 19.B.	Length 6 1/2"
2.	5449. E.R.1380K – 19.B.	Length 3 1/2"
3.	5447. E.R.1371E – 19.B.	Length 3 3/4"
4.	5657. E.R.1360B – 19.B.	Length 3 1/8"
41, No. 1.	5428. E.R.1368P – 19.B.	Length 4""
2.	5429. E.R.1323P – 19.B.	Length 4 1/2"
42.	5514. E.R.1385C – 19.B.	Ht. 7 3/4"
43.	5572. E.R.1331F – 19.B.	Length 20 1/2"
44.	5498. E.R.1369D – 19.B.	Diam. of Shot 1/8" and 3/16"
45.	5513. E.R.1362C – 19.B.	Length 1 1/4"